Top NBA Finals

BY RYAN JAMES

A Stingray Book

SEAHORSE PUBLISHING

Teaching Tips for Caregivers and Teachers:

This Hi-Lo book features high-interest subject matter that will appeal to all readers in intermediate and middle school grades. It may be enjoyed by students reading at or above grade level as well as by those who are looking for age-appropriate themes matched with a less challenging reading level. Hi-Lo books are ideal for ELL readers, too.

Each book appeals to a striving reader's age and maturity level. Opportunities are provided for students to read words they already know while encountering a limited number of new, high-interest vocabulary words. With these supports in place, students will read more fluently while increasing reading comprehension. Use the following suggestions to help students grow as readers.

- Encourage the student to read independently at home.
- Encourage the student to practice reading aloud.
- Encourage activities that require reading.
- Establish a regular reading time.
- Have the student write questions about what they read.

Teaching Tips for Teachers:

Before Reading

- Ask, "What do I know about this topic?"
- Ask, "What do I want to learn about this topic?"

During Reading

- Ask, "What is the author trying to teach me?"
- Ask, "How is this like something I already know?"

After Reading

- Discuss how the text features (headings, index, etc.) help with understanding the topic.
- Ask, "What interesting or fun fact did you learn?"

TABLE OF CONTENTS

WHAT ARE THE NBA FINALS?

The NBA Finals is a **series** of up to seven games that decides the champion of the NBA (National Basketball Association). The games are played each year between the winners of the Western and Eastern Conferences.

The first team to win four games is the champion.

The first NBA Finals took place in 1950 when the Minneapolis Lakers defeated the Syracuse Nationals.

FUN FACT: The current trophy is named after the third NBA commissioner, Larry O'Brien.

1957 NBA Finals

BOSTON

March 30 to April 13

BOSTON CELTICS	4	3	ST. LOUIS HAWKS

BOSTON GARDEN, BOSTON, MASSACHUSETTS
and KIEL AUDITORIUM, ST. LOUIS, MISSOURI

In game four, the Celtics tied up the series with a 123 to 118 win in St. Louis.

Returning to Boston, the Celtics won game five 124 to 109.

The Hawks came back to win game six 96 to 94, forcing a game seven. In double **overtime**, the Celtics won 125 to 123.

FUN FACT: The MVP (Most Valuable Player) trophy for the NBA Finals was first awarded in 1969.

1988 NBA Finals

June 7 to June 21

LOS ANGELES LAKERS	4	3	DETROIT PISTONS

THE FORUM, INGLEWOOD, CALIFORNIA
and THE PONTIAC SILVERDOME, PONTIAC, MICHIGAN

In game four, the Pistons beat the Lakers 111 to 86 to tie the series.

The Pistons came on strong to win game five.

During game six, Pistons **guard** Isiah Thomas sprained his ankle, but continued to play. He broke the record for scoring the most points during one quarter of the NBA Finals.

The final game went down to the wire, but the Lakers came out on top 108 to 105.

MOST VALUABLE PLAYER:
JAMES WORTHY

2010 NBA Finals

June 3 to June 17

LOS ANGELES LAKERS	4	3	BOSTON CELTICS

STAPLES CENTER, LOS ANGELES, CALIFORNIA and TD GARDEN, BOSTON, MASSACHUSETTS

The back-and-forth series had alternating wins. Game seven would decide the champion.

The Lakers led by six points with less than two minutes left. Boston's Rasheed Wallace sunk a three-point shot to cut the lead. With 11 seconds left, Celtics guard Rajon Rondo missed a shot. The Laker's Pau Gasol got the **rebound** and passed it to Lamar Odom. Odom lobbed the ball to the end of the court as the buzzer sounded.

This was the last NBA Finals win for basketball great Kobe Bryant.

MOST VALUABLE PLAYER:
KOBE BRYANT

2005 NBA Finals

June 9 to June 23

SAN ANTONIO SPURS	4	3	DETROIT PISTONS

SBC CENTER, SAN ANTONIO, TEXAS
and PALACE OF AUBURN HILLS, AUBURN HILLS, MICHIGAN

The Spurs won the first two games by double digits. Detroit had double-digit victories of their own in games three and four. The Spurs won game five in overtime.

The Pistons came back to win game six and force a seventh game.

Game seven was close until the fourth quarter. The Spurs charged ahead and became NBA Champions with a win 81 to 74.

Robert Horry became the second player to play on championship teams for three different teams.

MOST VALUABLE PLAYER:

TIM DUNCAN

1998 NBA Finals

June 3 to June 14

CHICAGO BULLS	4	2	UTAH JAZZ

UNITED CENTER, CHICAGO, ILLINOIS
and DELTA CENTER, SALT LAKE CITY, UTAH

The Jazz won game one in overtime. The Bulls had victories in the next three games. The Jazz won game five to force a sixth game.

With one minute left, Bulls guard Michael Jordan tied the game. John Stockton made a three-point shot, and the Jazz took the lead. Then, Jordan made a **layup**. It was now a one-point game.

Jordan stole the ball from Stockton and hit a 20-foot (six-meter) shot to take the lead for the Bulls.

This was the last championship game for legendary player Michael Jordan, who retired in 1999.

MOST VALUABLE PLAYER:

MICHAEL JORDAN

2016 NBA Finals

June 2 to June 19

CLEVELAND CAVALIERS	4	3	GOLDEN STATE WARRIORS

ORACLE ARENA, OAKLAND, CALIFORNIA
and QUICKEN LOANS ARENA, CLEVELAND, OHIO

The Cavaliers tied up the series by winning games five and six.

For the first time in NBA history, game seven began with both teams having scored the same number of total points during the first six games.

With less than one minute left in the game, Cavaliers point guard Kyrie Irving made a three-point **field goal** over the Warriors' Stephen Curry.

The Cavaliers got a 93 to 89 victory.

MOST VALUABLE PLAYER:

LEBRON JAMES

2013 NBA Finals

June 6 to June 20

MIAMI HEAT	4	3	SAN ANTONIO SPURS

AMERICAN AIRLINES ARENA, MIAMI, FLORIDA and AT&T CENTER, SAN ANTONIO, TEXAS

The Spurs set the NBA Finals record for most three-point shots in a game to win game three 113 to 77. The Heat came back in game four and won 109 to 93 to even the series.

Even though LeBron James and Dwyane Wade each scored 25 points for the Heat, the Spurs won game five 114 to 104.

Game six, when Ray Allen's three-point shot for the Heat forced the game into overtime, is considered one of the greatest games in NBA history.

MOST VALUABLE PLAYER:

LEBRON JAMES

1984 NBA Finals

May 27 to June 12

BOSTON CELTICS	4	3	LOS ANGELES LAKERS

BOSTON GARDEN, BOSTON, MASSACHUSETTS and THE FORUM, INGLEWOOD, CALIFORNIA

With an NBA Finals record of 21 **assists**, Magic Johnson helped the Lakers easily win game three.

The Celtics won games four and five. The Lakers came back in game six to tie the series.

With one minute left in game seven, Cedric Maxwell knocked the ball away from Magic Johnson. To seal the win, Celtics guard Dennis Johnson sunk two **free throws**.

This was the eighth time that the Celtics and Lakers played each other in the NBA Finals.

MOST VALUABLE PLAYER:

LARRY BIRD

GLOSSARY

assists (uh-SISTS): acts of one player helping another, especially to score points

field goal (feeld gohl): in basketball, a basket made when the ball is in play, scoring two or three points

free throws (free throhz): unhindered shots in basketball awarded because of a foul by an opponent

guard (gahrd): a basketball player whose job is often to initiate plays; there are point guards and shooting guards

layup (LAY-uhp): a basketball shot made with one hand from under the basket or from one side of the basket

overtime (OH-vur-time): extra time added to a game because the score was tied at the end of normal play

rebound (ree-BOUND): getting hold of a basketball after a missed shot, often after it has bounced off the backboard or rim

series (SEER-eez): a group of events that come one after the other

INDEX

AFTER READING QUESTIONS

1. How many games in the series must a team win to be the NBA Champion?
2. Which two teams played in the 2016 NBA Finals?
3. How many times had the Lakers and the Celtics met each other in the NBA Finals by 1984?
4. What NBA record did Isiah Thomas break in 1988?
5. How many points did LeBron James score in game five of the 2013 NBA Finals?

About the Author

Ryan James lives in the western part of North Carolina with his dog Bailey. As a child, he would go to Bobcats games with his dad while wearing the jersey of his favorite player, Gerald Wallace. When it's not basketball season, Ryan goes hiking and biking in the mountains.

Written by: Ryan James
Cover Design by: Rhea Magaro-Wallace
Interior Design by: Kathy Walsh
Editor: Kim Thompson

Library of Congress PCN Data
Top NBA Finals / Ryan James
Top Sports Championships
ISBN 978-1-63897-483-3 (hard cover)
ISBN 978-1-63897-598-4 (paperback)
ISBN 978-1-63897-713-1 (EPUB)
ISBN 978-1-63897-828-2 (eBook)
Library of Congress Control Number: 2022933972

Printed in the United States of America.

Photographs/Shutterstock: Cover ©winui, ©Nhat V. Meyer; Title Pg ©winui, ©EFKS; Pg 3 ©EFKS; Pg 4, 6, 8, 10, 12, 14, 16, 18, 20 ©Sedulur Grafis; Pg 7, 9, 11, 13, 15, 17, 19, 21 ©Little_Monster_2070, ©Sakina Xalilova; Pg 5 ©RAY CHAVEZ; Pg 6 ©javarman, ©Miceking, ©Public domain, via Wikimedia Commons; Pg 8 ©Detroit News; Pg 10 ©Kevin Sullivan; Pg 12 ©JULIAN H. GONZALEZ; Pg 14 ©NUCCIO DINUZZO; Pg 16 ©Prensa Internacional; Pg 18 ©Allen Eyestone; Pg 20 © Icon Sports Media, Inc. ;

Seahorse Publishing Company
www.seahorsepub.com

Published in the United States
Seahorse Publishing
PO Box 771325
Coral Springs, FL 33077

SEAHORSE PUBLISHING